Wisconsin

by the Capstone Press
Geography Department

Reading Consultant:
Peter O'Neil
Director of Instruction
Brodhead School District, Wisconsin

CAPSTONE PRESS
MANKATO, MINNESOTA

CAPSTONE PRESS
818 North Willow Street • Mankato, Minnesota 56001

Copyright © 1997 Capstone Press. All rights reserved. No part of this book may be reproduced without written permission from the publisher.

Printed in the United States of America.

Library of Congress Cataloging-in-Publication Data
   Wisconsin/by the Capstone Press Geography Department.
   p. cm.--(One Nation)
   Includes bibliographical references and index.
   Summary: Gives an overview of the state of Wisconsin, including its history, geography, people, and living conditions.
   ISBN 1-56065-5024-6
   1. Wisconsin--Juvenile literature. [1. Wisconsin.]
   I. Capstone Press. Geography Dept. II. Series.
F581.3.W57 1997
977.5--dc21

96-46848
CIP
AC

Photo credits
Root Resources/Lia Munson, cover; Jim Nachel, 21
Flag Research Center, 4 (left)
FPG, 28; Larry West, 4 (right), 5 (right); Gail Shumway, 8;
   James Blank, 12; Jerry Driendl, 16; Farrell Grehan, 30;
   Richard H. Smith, 32
Unicorn/Bill McMackins, 5 (left)
The House on the Rock, 6
Gary Nelson, 10, 22, 26
James Rowan, 18, 25, 34

Table of Contents

Fast Facts about Wisconsin 4

Chapter 1   The House on the Rock 7

Chapter 2   The Land 11

Chapter 3   The People 17

Chapter 4   Wisconsin History 23

Chapter 5   Wisconsin Business 31

Chapter 6   Seeing the Sights 35

Wisconsin Time Line 40

Famous Wisconsinites 42

Words to Know 44

To Learn More 45

Useful Addresses 46

Internet Sites 47

Index 48

Fast Facts about Wisconsin

State Flag

Location: In the Great Lakes region of the midwestern United States
Size: 56,154 square miles (146,000 square kilometers)

Population: 5,037,928 (1993 United States Census Bureau figures)
Capital: Madison
Date admitted to the Union: May 29, 1848; the 30th state

Robin

Wood violet

Largest cities: Milwaukee, Madison, Green Bay, Racine, Kenosha, Appleton, West Allis, Waukesha, Eau Claire, Oshkosh
Nickname: The Badger State
State animal: Badger
State bird: Robin
State flower: Wood violet
State tree: Sugar maple
State song: "On, Wisconsin!" by J. S. Hubbard, Charles D. Rosa, and William T. Purdy

Sugar maple

Chapter 1
The House on the Rock

One of Wisconsin's most unusual sites is the House on the Rock. It is built on a chimney rock. A chimney rock is a rock that stands out from the rest of the land and looks like a chimney. This rock is 60 feet (18 meters) tall. It is near the town of Spring Green.

Alex Jordan built this house in the 1940s. To build it, Jordan climbed a rope ladder. He carried baskets of stone and wood on his back.

The house has many levels. There are 14 rooms. The Infinity Room has 3,000 panels of glass. It juts out over the forest below.

The House on the Rock is one of Wisconsin's most unusual sites. It is near the town of Spring Green.

Wisconsinites were nicknamed after the badger.

Many other buildings are at ground level. They hold Jordan's many collections. There are miniature circuses, dolls, and firearms. One building houses a giant sculpture of a squid fighting a whale. Visitors can buy tokens to play music boxes that take up entire rooms. The world's largest carousel is also there. It has 269 different figures and 20,000 lights.

The Badger State
Not all Wisconsin homes are on rocks. In the 1820s, some lead miners dug holes in hillsides. They lived in those holes.

This reminded people of how badgers lived. Badgers dig underground tunnels. At first, only miners were called Badgers. Then the name was used for all Wisconsinites.

Something for Everyone
Millions of visitors come to Wisconsin each year. Many enjoy the state's farm country. They drive past herds of dairy cows. They stop in small towns to buy cheese.

Others visit Wisconsin's lakes and rivers. Many people tube down the Apple River. Some fish in the deep waters of Lake Superior and Lake Michigan.

Many people enjoy Wisconsin's winter sports. Snowmobilers cut trails through Wisconsin's North Woods. So do cross-country skiers. Downhill skiers enjoy skiing the slopes of Wisconsin's many small resorts.

Chapter 2
The Land

Wisconsin is in the Great Lakes region of the Midwest. Two of the Great Lakes touch Wisconsin. Lake Superior lies to the northwest. Lake Michigan is to the east.

Four midwestern states border Wisconsin. They are Illinois, Iowa, Minnesota, and Michigan.

Thousands of years ago, glaciers covered Wisconsin. These huge ice sheets scraped the land. They left behind lakes and streams.

The glaciers did not reach southwestern Wisconsin. Because of that, the land there is more uneven.

Lake Michigan borders Wisconsin on the east.

The Wisconsin Dells is a sandstone gorge.

The Northern Upland

The glaciers left thin and rocky soil in northern Wisconsin. Today forests cover most of this land. The Chequamegon National Forest is to the west. The Nicolet National Forest is in the east. The glaciers left thick, rich soil in the rest of the state.

The glaciers also left moraines. Moraines are rounded, rocky hills. Timms Hill is

Wisconsin's highest point. It reaches 1,952 feet (586 meters) above sea level.

Thousands of small lakes dot the uplands. Lake Chippewa and Lake Flambeau are large, artificially made lakes. These lakes were formed by dams.

The Central Plain

The Central Plain forms a V shape. It cuts through the middle of Wisconsin. Rolling hills cover the land. Fast-flowing rivers cross it.

Wisconsin Dells is at the V's southern tip. This popular tourist area is a sandstone gorge. A gorge is a narrow passage through steep walls of rocks. The Wisconsin River carved its cliffs.

The Western Upland

Small streams cut narrow valleys in southwestern Wisconsin. These streams empty into the Mississippi River.

Tall, beautiful bluffs line the Mississippi. They are made of sandstone and limestone.

Eastern Wisconsin

Rolling plains cover eastern Wisconsin. The state's richest soil is there. This area also has the state's longest growing season. Many farms dot the land.

Lake Winnebago is the largest lake within Wisconsin. The deepest one is Green Lake. Both lakes are in eastern Wisconsin.

Wisconsin's lowest point is along Lake Michigan. It is 581 feet (174 meters) above sea level.

Nine of Wisconsin's 10 biggest cities are in these lowlands. They include Milwaukee, Madison, Green Bay, Racine, and Kenosha.

Climate

Wisconsin has warm, humid summers. Humid means the air is heavy with moisture. Wisconsin's winters are long and cold. Temperatures are milder along Lake Michigan.

Snow falls heavily throughout the state. Northern Wisconsin can receive 100 inches (254 centimeters) of snow. About 30 inches (76 centimeters) of rain falls throughout the state every year. Wisconsin's trees and crops need this rain.

Wildlife

Northern Wisconsin's forests have black bears, deer, and foxes. Occasionally, people sight wolves and moose. Beavers and raccoons make their homes in the river valleys. Badgers are common in the south.

Muskellunges are huge game fish. They are usually called muskies. They swim in northern lakes. Pheasants, grouse, and ducks are some of Wisconsin's game birds.

Chapter 3

The People

Few people live in the state's northern half. More than 60 percent of Wisconsinites live in eastern Wisconsin.

Wisconsin's first settlers lived in the east. The land there was easy to farm. Good ports lay on Lake Michigan. Cities sprang up along the lake. Some of them were Manitowoc, Milwaukee, and Kenosha.

Today 66 percent of Wisconsinites live in cities. Only 34 percent live in rural areas.

Wisconsinites come from all over the world. However, almost 92 percent of them have European backgrounds.

Today 66 percent of Wisconsinites live in cities such as Milwaukee.

Some of Wisconsin's first settlers had Irish backgrounds. They built railroads throughout the state.

European Backgrounds

Some of Wisconsin's first settlers came from eastern states. Others came from southern states. The settlers' ancestors were English, Irish, and German.

Many European immigrants came directly to Wisconsin. Immigrants are people who come to another country to settle. Miners arrived from Cornwall, England. They settled in Mineral Point in the 1830s.

Later, German farmers arrived. Norwegians set up farms near Mount Horeb. Swedish people settled in the St. Croix Valley. New Glarus was home to Swiss people. Danish people settled in Racine.

Irish people built railroads in Wisconsin. Polish and Italian people worked in Milwaukee. Finnish and Russian people settled in northern Wisconsin.

Many of these ethnic groups still live in the same areas. Little Norway is a museum near Mount Horeb. The Swiss Volksfest takes place in New Glarus each August.

African Americans

About 5 percent of Wisconsinites are African American. Many live in cities in the south and east. Milwaukee has the state's largest African-American population.

African Americans began moving to Milwaukee in the 1920s. They worked in the city's factories and mills.

Every year, Milwaukee's African Americans celebrate their heritage. They hold the African World Festival. The festival offers food, music, and an African marketplace.

Native Americans

About 40,000 Native Americans live in Wisconsin. The largest tribe is the Ojibwa. The Oneida, Winnebago, and Menominee live in Wisconsin also.

There are 11 reservations in the state. A reservation is land set aside for use by Native Americans. The Menominee have the largest one. Ojibwa reservations are in northern Wisconsin. They include Lac Courte Oreilles, Lac Du Flambeau, and Red Cliff.

Hispanic Americans

Almost 2 percent of Wisconsinites are Hispanic. They speak Spanish or have Spanish-speaking backgrounds. Most Hispanics in Wisconsin came from Mexico.

The first Mexicans in Wisconsin were migrant farm workers. Migrants are people who move to do seasonal work. Now most Hispanics live in Wisconsin's cities. They work in factories. Some Hispanics have started their own businesses.

The Menominee have the largest reservation in Wisconsin. They celebrate their culture by having powwows.

Asian Americans

About 1 percent of Wisconsinites are Asian American. Milwaukee has Vietnamese, Chinese, Japanese, and Cambodian families. About 7,000 people from India live in the state.

Wisconsin's largest Asian group is the Hmong. They came from northern Laos. Almost 17,000 Hmong live in Wisconsin.

Chapter 4

Wisconsin History

Wisconsin's first people probably arrived about 10,000 years ago. By 500 B.C., mound builders lived in Wisconsin. They built huge dirt mounds.

Some mounds were shaped like snakes and birds. One mound stills stands at Lizard Mound Park. This is near West Bend.

Native Americans Arrive

By the 1600s, many Native Americans had moved to Wisconsin. The Winnebago lived near Green Bay. The Menominee lived in the northeastern hills. The Dakotas settled in the northwest.

In the 1600s, Native Americans lived on the unspoiled lands of Wisconsin.

Later, the Ojibwa came. They hunted and fished along Lake Superior. Sauk, Fox, and Potawatomi also lived in Wisconsin.

French and English Claims

Jean Nicolet came to Wisconsin from French Canada in 1634. He landed on the shore of Green Bay. Nicolet was the first European to see Wisconsin.

French traders came later. They exchanged goods with Native Americans. In return, the traders received furs.

French missionaries also arrived. Missionaries are people sent to do religious or charitable work in a territory or foreign country. The missionaries taught Native Americans about Christianity.

England already had 13 colonies. They were on the Atlantic Ocean. In 1763, England gained the French lands. Wisconsin became an English territory, too.

Wisconsin Becomes U.S. Property

In 1775, the 13 English colonies went to war against England. The colonists wanted their

Jean Nicolet landed on the shore of Green Bay in 1634.

Many settlers came from other states to farm in Wisconsin.

own government. This Revolutionary War ended in 1783.

The United States won its independence. It also gained all of England's land east of the Mississippi, including Wisconsin.

Becoming a State

Settlers came from eastern and southern states. Lead miners arrived in southwestern Wisconsin. Farmers lived on land in the east.

Native Americans still lived in Wisconsin. The settlers pushed them from the land. The United States Army defeated the Winnebago in 1827. The Sauk and Fox were defeated in 1832. That ended the Black Hawk War (1832).

Thousands of Americans then rushed into Wisconsin. Even more came from Europe. In the 1840s, Wisconsin had 200,000 people. That was more than enough for statehood.

On May 29, 1848, Wisconsin joined the United States. It became the 30th state. Madison was the capital.

The Fight Against Slavery
In the 1850s, slavery was tearing the United States apart. The southern states still allowed slavery. Wisconsin and other northern states had banned it.

In 1854, anti-slavery leaders met in Ripon, Wisconsin. They started the Republican party. Abraham Lincoln became a Republican. He was elected president in 1860.

In 1861, the Civil War started. About 90,000 Wisconsinites fought on the side of the northern states. The South surrendered in 1865. Slavery ended in the United States.

Robert M. La Follett Sr. (center) started the Progressive party. He ran for the office of President of the United States.

New Industries

In the 1870s, lumbering started in Wisconsin. Lumberjacks cut down millions of trees. Whole forests disappeared in northern Wisconsin. In 1900, Wisconsin led the states in lumbering.

In the 1880s, new companies opened in Wisconsin. They made goods from Wisconsin's trees. Some made furniture and wagons. Others made paper from wood pulp. Thousands of people came to work in Wisconsin's factories.

The Progressive Years

In 1904, Robert M. La Follette Sr. started a new political party. It was called the Progressive party.

La Follette served as Wisconsin's governor from 1901 to 1906. He brought changes for Wisconsin's workers. The state set a minimum wage. Retired workers drew state pensions.

The Great Depression

The Great Depression (1929-1939) hit the entire nation. Many Milwaukee factories closed. Wisconsin farmers lost their land.

Governor Philip La Follette Jr. helped Wisconsin's people. The jobless received money from the state. Wisconsin was the first state to do that. The state also created new jobs. Workers helped build new roads in Wisconsin.

Wisconsin Today

In the 1990s, Governor Tommy Thompson started welfare reform. People on welfare had to get job training and find work.

Also in the 1990s, Wisconsin became a leader in agribusiness. Agribusiness means jobs related to farming. They include growing better crops, making food, and selling special dairy equipment.

Chapter 5
Wisconsin Business

Wisconsin started as a mining and farming state. Lumbering became important, too.

By the 1950s, Wisconsin had become a manufacturing center. Manufacturing is still one of the state's largest businesses.

Service industries, however, are now Wisconsin's biggest business. Tourism and trade are important Wisconsin services.

Manufacturing
Southeastern Wisconsin cities make machinery. Engines and appliances come from their factories. They also build cars and parts for cars.

Manufacturing is an important Wisconsin business. The S. C. Johnson Wax building in Racine was designed by the famous Wisconsin architect, Frank Lloyd Wright.

Food processing is a big Wisconsin business. The state is a leading maker of cheese.

Food processing is also a big business. Dairy foods lead the way. Wisconsin makes more butter than any other state. It is a leading maker of cheese, too.

Wisconsin also has large meat-packing plants. The state is a leader in canning foods. Some of these foods are peas, sweet corn, and cranberries.

La Crosse and Milwaukee have breweries. They ship beer throughout the country.

Green Bay has paper factories. Northern Wisconsin also has many lumber mills.

Service Industries

Visitors to Wisconsin spend about $6 billion each year. Resorts along the state's lakes make much of this money. Other dollars are spent at restaurants and hotels.

Trade takes place throughout the state. Goods are shipped into and out of Wisconsin. Much of this takes place in its port cities. Superior, Green Bay, and Milwaukee are leading ports.

Agriculture and Forestry

Wisconsin's most important kind of farming is dairy farming. Wisconsin's cows produce the most milk of all the states.

Many farmers also raise hogs, beef cattle, and chickens. Eggs are another important farm product.

Corn is the state's leading crop. Wisconsin farmers also raise soybeans, snap beans, peas, and cranberries.

Forestry is also a big business in northern Wisconsin. Loggers cut ash, pine, maple, and oak trees.

Chapter 6

Seeing the Sights

Wisconsin has many great sights. Its forests, lakes, and rivers offer outdoor fun. Its big cities have museums and zoos. Wisconsin's small towns are fun, too.

The North Woods
Bayfield is in the far northern tip of Wisconsin. It is on Lake Superior. The town is known for its whitefish.

Offshore are the 22 Apostle Islands. About 150 people live on Madeline Island. A ferry takes visitors from Bayfield to Madeline. The other islands are set aside for animals. Nothing can be built by humans on those islands.

The Ringling Brothers Circus started in Baraboo in 1884.

To the south is the Chequamegon National Forest. Many lakes are in these woods. Some people fish for walleye and bass there. Others hunt for deer and bear.

Northern Wisconsin has great winter fun. The Snowmobile Racing Hall of Fame is in Eagle River. This snow-covered town hosts the World Championship Snowmobile Derby every January.

The American Birkebeiner is run each February. This is a 34-mile (54-kilometer) race. It is done on cross-country skis. More than 6,000 skiers start in Hayward. They end in Cable. These towns are in northwestern Wisconsin.

Northeastern Wisconsin

The Door County peninsula lies in far northeastern Wisconsin. No county in the nation has more coastline.

Many visitors stop in Sturgeon Bay. There they can watch ships and boats being built.

In the south end of the peninsula is Green Bay. This city is home to the Green Bay

Packers. Fans visit the Packer Hall of Fame. It honors Packer football players.

Central Wisconsin

Manitowoc is on Lake Michigan. The Maritime Museum is there. It displays the USS *Cobia*. This is a World War II (1939-1945) submarine.

East of Manitowoc is Oshkosh. A popular clothing company is there.

La Crosse is on the western edge of the state. This town is on the Mississippi River. Many people go sightseeing along the river. They can take a ride on a paddle-wheel riverboat.

Around the Dells

The Wisconsin Dells is a resort town. It lies on both sides of the Wisconsin River.

Visitors to the Dells can ride the Wisconsin Ducks. These are old military vehicles. They can travel both on land and in water. The Ducks carry tourists along the Wisconsin River. Visitors can see sandstone cliffs carved by the river.

Baraboo is nearby. The Ringling Brothers Circus started there in 1884. Today, Baraboo has the Circus World Museum. Live circus shows still take place there.

Spring Green is southwest of Baraboo. Frank Lloyd Wright, a famous architect, grew up there. Taliesin was his home. He built the house in his Prairie Style. The rooms are long and low. The house blends in with the nearby land.

Madison

Madison is in the middle of southern Wisconsin. It sits between Lake Monona and Lake Mendota. Madison is the state's second largest city. It is also the state capital.

Madison is home to the University of Wisconsin. More than 50,000 students go to school there. Wisconsin sports fans cheer for the school's Badger teams.

Milwaukee

Milwaukee is in southeastern Wisconsin. It is on Lake Michigan. Milwaukee is Wisconsin's biggest city. It is a major Great Lakes port.

Milwaukee's people enjoy acres of parks. Whitnall Park has a golf course, botanical gardens, and a nature center. Some parks are along the lake.

Frederick Pabst owned a large Milwaukee brewery. He built two Milwaukee landmarks. Today, plays are still performed in the Pabst Theater. The Pabst Mansion is open to the public. It is an example of how rich people lived in the 1890s.

Grown-ups and children love the Milwaukee County Zoo. It is one of the nation's best-known zoos.

Wisconsin Time Line

10,000 B.C.—The first people begin arriving in Wisconsin.

500 B.C.—Mound builders make huge earth mounds.

A.D. 1600—Menominee, Dakota, and Winnebago people live in Wisconsin.

1634—Explorer Jean Nicolet lands on the shores of Green Bay.

1671-1763—The French control Wisconsin.

1763—The English gain control of Wisconsin.

1783—The United States gains control of Wisconsin.

1832—The Fox and Sauk are defeated, ending the Black Hawk War.

1836—Wisconsin becomes a United States territory.

1848—Wisconsin becomes the 30th state.

1854—Anti-slavery leaders form the Republican party in Ripon.

1856—Margarethe Schurz opens the nation's first kindergarten in Watertown.

1871—About 1,200 people die in the Peshtigo Fire.

1901—Robert M. La Follette Sr. becomes governor and begins an era of Progressive reforms.

1932—Wisconsin passes the nation's first law for states to provide money to unemployed people.

1957—The Milwaukee Braves win the World Series.

1966 and 1967—The Green Bay Packers win the first two Super Bowls.

1971—The Milwaukee Bucks win the NBA championship.

1982—A project to rebuild downtown Milwaukee is completed.

1994—The University of Wisconsin wins the Rose Bowl.

1996—Shirley Abrahamson becomes the first woman chief justice of the Wisconsin Supreme Court.

Famous Wisconsinites

Seymour Cray (1925-1996) Computer wizard who developed supercomputers; born in Chippewa Falls.

Ada Deer (1935-) Native American rights activist who helped regain lands for the Menominee; born on the Menominee Indian Reservation.

Jeane Dixon (1918-) Astrologer and newspaper columnist; born in Medford.

Eric Heiden (1958-) Speed skater who won five gold medals at the 1980 Winter Olympics; born in Madison.

Robert M. La Follette Sr. (1855-1925) Wisconsin's governor (1901-1906); founder of the Progressive party in 1904; won 17 percent of the vote in the 1924 presidental race; born in Primrose.

Joseph McCarthy (1908-1957) United States senator from Wisconsin (1947-1957) who led an investigation of Communists in the 1950s; born in Grand Chute.

Golda Meir (1898-1978) Teacher and politician who grew up and taught in Milwaukee before becoming Israel's first woman prime minister.

Georgia O'Keeffe (1887-1986) Artist best known for her desert landscapes; born in Sun Prairie.

William Rehnquist (1924-) U.S. Supreme Court Justice (1971-1986); became the chief justice in 1986; born in Milwaukee.

Tom Snyder (1936-) Radio and television talk-show host; born in Milwaukee.

Orson Welles (1915-1985) Actor and filmmaker; born in Kenosha.

Gene Wilder (1935-) Actor in *Willy Wonka and the Chocolate Factory*; born in Milwaukee.

Laura Ingalls Wilder (1867-1957) Novelist who wrote the Little House books; born in Pepin.

Frank Lloyd Wright (1867-1959) Architect who developed the Prairie Style for homes in the Midwest; born in Richland Center.

Words to Know

ancestor—a person from whom one is descended
carousel—a merry-go-round with carved wooden horses or other animals that move up and down
ethnic group—people with a common culture
glacier—a huge sheet of slowly moving ice
gorge—a narrow passage through steep walls of rock
growing season—the number of days each year during which crops can grow
immigrant—a person who comes to another country to settle
migrant—a person who moves to do seasonal work
missionary—a person who is sent to do religious or charitable work in a territory or foreign country
moraine—a rocky, rounded hill created by glaciers
museum—a place in which interesting or valuable objects are displayed
reform—a change made to improve some part of government, the economy, or society
reservation—land set aside for use by Native Americans
rural—relating to farm areas and small towns
surrender—to give up

welfare—a system of payments from the government to the unemployed or poor

To Learn More

Aylesworth, Thomas G. and Virginia L. Aylesworth. *Western Great Lakes.* New York: Chelsea House, 1992.

Blashfield, Jean F., Margie Benson, and Nancy Jacobson. *Awesome Almanac: Wisconsin.* Fontana, Wis.: B & B Publishing, 1993.

Fradin, Dennis B. *Wisconsin.* Sea to Shining Sea. Chicago: Children's Press, 1992.

Stan, Susan. *The Objiwe.* Native American People. Vero Beach, Fla.: Rourke Publications, 1989.

Stein, R. Conrad. *Wisconsin.* America the Beautiful. Chicago: Children's Press, 1992.

Useful Addresses

Cave of the Mounds
Brigham Farm
Blue Mounds, WI 53517

Chalet Cheese Co-op
N4858 County Highway N
Monroe, WI 53566

Chippewa Moraine Ice Age Interpretive Center
13394 County Highway M
New Auburn, WI 54757

Circus World Museum
426 Water Street
Baraboo, WI 53913

House on the Rock
5754 Highway 23
Spring Green, WI 53588

Mitchell Park Horticultural Conservatory
524 South Layton Boulevard
Milwaukee, WI 53215

National Railroad Museum
2285 South Broadway
Green Bay, WI 54304

Internet Sites

City.Net Wisconsin
http://city.net/countries/united_states/wisconsin

Travel.org—Wisconsin
http://travel.org/wisconsi.html

State of Wisconsin
http://www.state.wi.us

Quirky Destinations
http://badger.state.wi.us/agencies/tourism/guide/destin00.htm

Index

African World Festival, 19
Apostle Islands, 35
Apple River, 9

badger, 5, 9, 15
Black Hawk War, 27

cheese, 9, 32
Chequamegon National Forest, 12, 36

Door County, 36

Green Bay, 5, 23-24, 33, 36

House on the Rock, 7

Jordan, Alex, 7

La Follette, Philip, 29
La Follette, Robert M., 29
Lake Michigan, 9, 11, 14, 17, 37
Lake Superior, 9, 11, 24, 35
Lincoln, Abraham, 27
Lizard Mounds National Park, 23

lumbering, 28, 31, 33

Madison, 4-5, 14, 27, 38
Menominee, 20, 23
Milwaukee, 5, 14, 17, 19, 32-33, 38-39
moraine, 12
muskie, 15

Nicolet, Jean, 24

Ojibwa, 20, 24

Packers, 37

Racine, 5, 19
Ringling Brothers Circus, 37

Spring Green, 7

Thompson, Tommy, 29
Timms Hill, 12
Volksfest, 19

Wisconsin Dells, 13, 37
Wright, Frank Lloyd, 38